Singer, An Elegy

Singer, An Elegy

George Fetherling

ANVIL PRESS | VANCOUVER

Singer, an elegy
Copyright © 2004 by George Fetherling

LIBRARY AND ARCHIVES CANADA CATALOGUING IN PUBLICATION
Fetherling, George.
Singer, an elegy / George Fetherling.

Poetry.
ISBN: 1-895636-63-9 (BOUND). —ISBN: 1-895636-61-2 (PBK.)
I. Title
PS8561.E834S55 2004   C811'.54   C2004-904668-3

Printed and bound in Canada by Houghton Boston Printers
Cover design: Rayola Graphic Design

Represented in Canada by the Literary Press Group
Distributed by the University of Toronto Press

The publisher gratefully acknowledges the financial assistance of
the B.C. Arts Council, the Canada Council for the Arts, and the Department
of Canadian Heritage through the Book Publishing Industry Development
Program (BPIDP) for their support of our publishing program.

Anvil Press
P.O. Box 3008,
MAIN POST OFFICE
Vancouver, BC
V6B 3X5

"Most funerals are insults; they belittle the dead. If anything should be honest a funeral should be honest."
— *Walt Whitman to Horace Traubel,*
11 June 1888

"Death is like being invited out to a good dinner."
— *Walt Whitman to Horace Traubel,*
5 February 1889

Following a bridge is like following a river:
you can't possibly get lost.

You begin in one place and end somewhere else.
Years ago, before the bridge opened,

the dead used to cross by ferry.
Anonymity was valued as a preview back then.

There was no language to speak
of, so no one spoke of it. ~

He stopped when the music stopped
stopped when the night stopped.

Memory is the last surviving document.
Hearsay evidence is all I hear said

inside the night-silence when
important stuff rises to the surface at last.

Hard to judge what number he'd been given
as all those files have disappeared.

Hard to know where he was slotted in the world
he loved, sensing how the past's decay

makes the present's possible—"a wide-open town"
he could get in step with.

The moderns fought for fun with
blood the prize.

The map was a tall isosceles triangle.
He felt at home between its wide shoulders

in old frame houses and in factories and plants
with their names in black block letters

on white rectangles painted on the dirty bricks:
MILLING & MACHINE—SOUTH END WORKS.

Miles were longer then and cities in motion
and that which he knew, he knew.

I suppose he was a bit like Thoreau who
"travelled widely in Concord"

but his style was more Whitman, a machine man
who liked to get his hands dirty learning

how things worked. He cleaned
and embellished in a single motion,

hiding some facts, discovering others.
"Nobody's any the wiser."

I can't know if he was depressed
because he had just one mood (happy enough)

and only one mode (getting along fine
in the circumstances).

He perfected the etiquette
of letting others think he wasn't all

that complex. With such filters he couldn't
be buffaloed.

Many were fooled but others weren't,
detecting a style of being in the world

like the trace of some outgrown accent
hinting at higher expectations

abandoned overthrown ignored renounced.
Nouns say no more than verbs:

self-destruction exile bad luck asceticism
hard-times gumption peace and quiet

get-up-and-go.
He was of a different syntactical type

dreaming adjectives but living adverbs
so that most of what I know of him

I've learned from myself by myself.
The mirror compares unfavourably

with seventy-year-old snapshots
and my ignorance is no less anguished.

I think of him photographing a buddy of his
then turning the camera on himself.

A click rings out.
An image falls to the ground. ~

What to do first after checking in.
Put cash in hotel safe (no credit

cards back then), tip
bellhop who carried the bags

to bring up some mixer and ice.
He knew how to pack a suitcase

so nothing got wrinkled and the
bottle never broke:

another survival of his young
life on the road when nights

clicked past Pullman car windows
like the sound of someone

playing castanets.
Canadian Club whisky,

pasteboard suitcase with corners
reinforced with rivets worn

shiny smooth like the pads
on an old dog's paws.

Clothes, folded inside, like
himself of good quality and

a generation out of date.
He didn't live to see them

or himself revived
but in the sadness of

retrospective vision I see
us growing daily more alike

to the point where two images
superimposed become one

face, each layer making
the other sharper.

I inherit his comfort there
but hotels are different now, more

Japanese by the minute,
short-time storage for the nameless,

no cast of passion players changing
with each performance and

every word spoken or sung.
What's to be found in the world

he'd grown up in and sometimes
was allowed to revisit a few days

a few nights here and there—
cigar-stands in lobbies, newsstands

in lobbies too, elevator
operators, a liveried boy calling

out the names of guests with messages waiting,
maybe that redheaded manicurist (charm

is situational that way)?
Last thing before retiring is

place shoes outside door to
be collected and returned all polished

by somebody no one's ever seen.
He was a modernist angel, what

more can I say? That explains
everything, something, nothing at all. ~

List of singers and actors he liked.
Louis Armstrong

but also Dean Martin
Louis Prima

Phil Harris
Jack Webb

Jackie Gleason
cool nightclub characters

tuxedos with the ties undone
smoking cigarettes

small talents wasted
not needing to say they grew

up in the Thirties because it showed
in what their faces hid.

Singers and actresses he liked.
Peggy Lee

Lola Albright
Diana Dors (why not Marilyn Monroe?)

a full cast, subject to change,
mostly private.

When I was a kid he read to me
from Tallulah Bankhead's autobiography.

"That explains a lot," a woman once said
when I told her this

which of course says nothing
about me (I'm simply the lector here). ~

He has visited others who loved
him less, why not me?

My receiver is to blame, not his signal;
I'm sensitive in ways of no use to anyone.

If he had lived longer or I'd grown faster
we could have intersected outside science.

He might have imparted what he kept
out of sight except when alone with someone

the same age,
dropping little clues to test for sympathy

and loyalty, probing
to find out if the other fellow too

used language for speaking:
two wide-tie survivors in a narrow-tie world

soon to be no-tie at all,
communication reduced to

simple pictures and cities destroyed
leaving beautiful ruins sometimes.

How could he live so few years yet
still be an exile from the past?

When he knew me, I couldn't have
formed the answer

or even understood the question.
In poems of a certain type the last

line should always be first.
Dreams nag, art pleads. Deaths

make poetry inadequate, especially
the worst kind when you die

rigid in fear, the body going dark
while the lights still burn: death

all out of proportion to what's
taken place so far.

The path of recollection is along a dark
hallway past a tall-case clock

whose hands have razor edges.
Every tick is a chop of the axe.

Withdrawing becomes an exercise, a lesson
that can't be passed on.

All of us must learn it. Human life
isn't terribly efficient this way.

Biology is our fear,
geology our burden. ~

It's not that he had
no name, he had no

identity any longer
little choice in how things end.

Some decisions are made for him
slithering closer in his sleep

then draining energy through punctures in the night
while the rich live long to expire irreversibly

their death no holiday but the long relaxation.
There's also horror to take into account

the terror of being unprepared
which is maybe where he had the advantage

bred to death from birth
then finding Herschel, a failure in 1938, cold

in the cellar that he'd sought
to escape his English wife and sit

reading as he liked to do
beside a hogshead of premium whisky

he'd shepherded through the Depression:
Singer saw him there and afterwards

was approached in a dream
no vision, a visitation

so real he thought he touched the flesh
but what was being said?

That's what we've all been asking.
I'm listening hard, straining

no one tells me
anything anymore.

If you won't give me any answers
then at least let me broach the questions

I would have asked if you'd lived and I'd grown up.
Did you feel guilty to have missed the war?

what was that sensation in your chest you
always said was pleurisy?

what was it like to come home
to a house where no music was allowed

no books no love eating bad food
made with rancour and seasoned with hate

going to the movies once between
1949 and 1966 with even that provoking

the sort of outrage that always got
her banned and you along with her

from places of the lowest resort
until finally you'd sit parked in the car

listening without impression to her ignorant abuse
because no expression was allowed

and then when she'd gone, slamming the door
she both exited through and entered,

you'd still look beyond the windshield
towards the green and the grey, thinking

what exactly?
Fragments of the past were comforting.

He could remember riverboats and being a kid
in a city where the neighbourhoods were tribes. ~

He was patient with the present
no doubt too patient,

tolerant of the future
perhaps foolishly.

He kept the important
parts of the past to himself

where I couldn't find them
without knowing there were questions to ask

much less knowing the right ones.
For him, I believe, it all came down

to not having anyone to confide in,
only a superficial beer-joint buddy

and a kid too young to understand what
was going on.

But I sensed there were places
to know where even someone snooping

on his own dreams must make a selection
from all the disasters being offered.

If his life was like mine and other people's,
choices rushed up and completely filled

his field of vision and he reacted,
hoping for the best. Make the wrong

decision and choice recedes to a dot
that disappears. When nightmare

takes over the carnival midway,
the calliope plays screams. ~

To be eighteen then was to feel
cheated and be scared. That's how I imagine it

recalling that old mnemonic device—
unemployment hits 33 percent 1933.

But this is an aid to remembering what he
wished to forget but couldn't.

What little tricks do we use with ourselves
to disregard or ignore outright?

In this area he was blessed with riches
on whose interest I scrape by.

I also grieve because grief has defined
me this way with whatever strength I have.

I've remained an outsider among the dead
since we traded places—he leaving, I staying behind,

there's such a chilling neatness to
continuity of this sort.

Another grief requires a degree
of concentration I've never shown.

It's a state of awareness I've kept myself from
by doing whatever I've done. Now that I've determined

I failed, it flows back over me like a welcoming tide.
Who knew it could be this warm?

I feel completed by not being whole
and pray that for you the reverse is true.

This is as much philosophy as I know at present.
Nothing so far has compensated. Sometimes I distract

myself for a moment, nothing more.
Am I worthy of what I feel?

The arithmetic of it is facile, but one
can't say glibly that the ground turned to quicksand

when he hit thirty and the soldiers came home.
What I hear are missteps well on their way to

becoming a run, a rout in fact,
in a lethal acceleration that could neither

be predicted nor stopped once underway
but withstood with a dignity that didn't seem

dignified to others more fortunate,
or less. It took courage

to look for past warmth when this morning was
worn and brown, to bum for work with a soft voice

and go on the road at two cents a mile
to the cities that drained the countryside

but also to towns no railway sought as you did
those restaurants Recommended by Duncan Hines

and other comforts along the highways
with motor courts spurned for a proper hotel.

Of course speed is courage especially to the young
but so is distance covered. Freedom is courage

and so is self-confinement.
Hotels can be courage

if you know how to use them.
They're part of a strategy.

At some stage death ceases to seem
such a distant epidemic

and so he died and in time
the city followed, money

getting scarce and crowds grown thin,
upper storeys abandoned first

(red Xs in never-washed windows
signifying vacancies),

then the rot crept lower until finally
the ground floor too is boarded up painted over

as though the owners could fool
us into believing they'd make a

fresh start when things got better.
Once he earned a living being young.

He never had the chance to earn a living being old.
In between, he made his own hand tools

which was cheaper than buying.
He had to be satisfied with the craft

when he used them to build machinery
that helped make more machinery.

The literal was also metaphor.
"He's a real piece of machinery, that one is!"

A character, a card. The heart is
an engine of sorts. "Be careful

when you give it the gun. You'll
flood it."

He got a friend to weld
a homemade hasp on the heavy tool chest

though it never knew a lock.
Snub-nose pliers and needle-nose pliers,

vice-grips, drills and bits,
a ball-peen hammer, scribers and punches,

files. A micrometer.
A small pair of bow-handled wire-strippers

with a quarter-inch wrench on the end of one arm.
He must have dreamed up that one

for a particular job and thought it too good to throw out.
He stencilled his initials on the head

of an eight-pound sledge and the handle
of a carpenter's saw. Other stuff.

Much other stuff.
There was a good-quality whetstone its original

cardboard box now frayed and below that folded clippings
from a "men's magazine." Something about the Quarter

in New Orleans and "the old Gaslight Club in Chicago"
where the women wore shoes net stockings and

nothing else. Finding these
a boy grew excited then sad

about rivers coming to an end in denial and frustration.
There were six, eight integrated mills making

steel from scratch not from other people's scrap.
At night the sky was orange in Aetnaville

so named by someone with a classical education
who also owned the whorehouses.

They were profitable in themselves and a necessary cost
of doing business to keep the hunkies happy

micks spics greaseballs they'd turn commie
in a minute unless kept busy fighting one another.

In wartime the plants went twenty-four hours:
three shifts. Men learned who was hiring the same way

packs of dogs learn where food is.
Now the centre was cooling and the edges

where he lived breaking away.
He'd rather be down in New Orleans

with chicory in the coffee, oysters for breakfast
if you wanted then apple pandowdy for dessert,

a band always playing just out of hearing and people
who know what decay is for, not up north

making his own tools like a slave
turned blacksmith shackling himself.

Baskets full of tools.
He needed a long life to live off such metal fruit. ~

Frozen bones cracked in winter
if you weren't careful in the dreams

of summer faraway when the tar
between the paving bricks might percolate

in streets so steep those houses walked
on stilts to be their neighbours' equal.

Evidence of some great defining prosperity
from his father's century

influenced silhouettes everywhere,
much as we grew up with traces

of his own time poking out between the slats
as others with practice can ignore

our towers decaying unfashionably,
a subtle irritation but constant.

Neighbourhoods gathered round churches
some with onion domes, most with steeples,

city of hat brims, overcoats, coffee-and-a-piece-of-pie,
bridges and the strange geometry of dusk,

dressed stone retaining walls failing to hold
everything in place,

lights distorted freaks in the dark water,
radiant specks in the dawn like dust

in a room on sunny afternoons and other colour
crimes disturbing a largely black-and-white world

as when liquid steel swaggered down the path
that nursed it, as though it were a brook

in the time before English or French
when the first hunters waited with dead-stone patience   33

where hustlers later prowled and cops gave in
to their suspicions:

city of lunch-pails burlesque houses taverns with jars
of pickled eggs, one was supposed to buy the boys a round

on payday every other Thursday and die where one was born
and once dead stay that way until the Day of Judgment

that never seemed to come: a city that
took root without enough soil to support it,

growth was upward and districts compact,
bankers and lawyers a bribe's distance from the courthouse,

men of business like his father on an outer ring
straining to persist, hoping to gain

going forward by looking neither up nor down
and then not looking back.

My conceit is that I can see the scene
as he and they might have done

with the streets changing hands at night
like a city on a frontier that's always in dispute.

Rules get suspended when the marquees come on.
He saw the crowds go in, saw them once more

whenever the shows let out.
I remember what it's like to be in nostalgia deficit.

What seemed to be a profession was merely
prophecy in reverse.

Life, being chronic, would never
improve. ~

I need to find the part of the story
that's the same for him as for me.

I have the setting but not the plot.
A "good burg" somewhere that he checks

into as he might check into exile
or a nicely anonymous hotel.

I know the opening too.
He arrives discreetly on an oblique train

that leaves the tunnel to enter the twilight.
He doesn't need to know anybody there.

In the brotherhood to which he subscribes
every man answers to Jasper, Sport, Jocko, Skipper.

"Who's that bird standing at the bar?"
The question need never come up in

a cocktail lounge at its darkest when
the sun is directly overhead.

He carries his own bag from station to bridge
past jailhouse, courthouse, department store

wholesale district, financial district, tenderloin.
He gets the goods on the place. He's already

got it all doped out.
How did he come by such rich gifts of knowledge

of what's behind the door down the alley,
who pulls the strings and who does

the bidding?
In a life of fear and boredom

he can at least do something about the boredom
and put up there for a while, a hideout in the open,

a city small enough that he can know it
but big enough so no one cares.

Forgive our eavesdropping
as we forgive those who eavesdrop against us.

There's no need to pretend to be tough.
It doesn't matter. Let others take care of that.

Nurse the hurt till it's better. Think this thing
through. At least come up

with the questions.
There are too many to list or even remember.

Many are trivial, a couple profound,
time has declawed most of the others

for people's messes usually die with them:
another dormant blessing.

My object is to see which ones have been
resolved and how, which are insoluble and why.

I've not been terribly successful so far.
Evidence piles up, meaning grows dimmer,

I'm writing this just in time.
Hindsight like this is a privilege of the living.

Dig in but not too deeply would have been
my advice. Don't get stuck there.

His comprehension travels. Stay loose
but keep alert. Leave false trails and be gone

before breakfast, just one more person
moving in and out of

a clockwork that doesn't tell time.
That's what people believed a city was. ~

When one of the fluorescent lights
grew old it made a sound like insects

buzzing then flickered then died.
The one on the left gave out often,

a short most likely congenital, so
he shaved with half his face in shadow,

the nicks on the skin making signs that said
one part of his body was already condemned

and the other condemned to follow.
He knew where the bootleggers went

for brewer's yeast in bricks
and he'd dissolve some in boiling water

to treat the infection in his poor inflamed lung
on the left side where the heart is. ~

All that can be expected is that
I know nothing more than what I recall

like a refugee who escapes without
a second to spare with not just

the clothes on his back but also
the pictures in his brain.

Who's to say who's wrong when
someone says Singer was a loser?

He was sly, plodding, delusional, grand,
even-tempered, doomed and resigned

to being doomed, romantic, linguistically playful,
probably always in poor health,

screwing up frequently and
sometimes he and I bonded by

screwing up together as
parents and children ought to do

never splashing the oil in the lamp
in their passion to hug the darkness. ~

What I took as stoic refusal was merely
the synopsis of dark and daylight;

only now do I start to recognise
the correspondence.

Herschel hid in his cellar from too much
unwavering gentility,

Singer in his from the evident monstrosity
of the one overhead

who escaped the backcountry longing
for the sidewalks he left for exile

in someplace well out of the sun.
She was a Forties person whom the war might rescue

though that's all she grasped of it.
(She once told me Hitler was a communist and

that's as much as she needed to know.)
He while younger was a Thirties type,

a New Dealer, a product more of ruin than decay
who found his family on the other side of the crevasse

once Earth broke apart right
where they were standing.

Everything conspired to wreck her mind
already weak. Alcohol begging the rage,

even poor eyesight urging paranoia;
they were depressed in incompatible ways.

She did not understand what was taking place
and turned violent like an animal

almost rabid. He sensed the presence of fate.
Luck created the problem, now let luck fix it,

allow events to resolve themselves,
inertia to run its course

without prejudice or external pressures.
I was caught in a marriage once, I understand

better now.
I remember him taking a long thin pole

to measure the level in the cisterns.
I remember how he ordered a ton of coal

delivered down the chute each autumn with a volcanic roar
and a large bloom of fine black powder.

Eventually the noise evaporated and the particles
in the air reunited with their source.

I see him stoking the furnace at five a.m.
sending the heat of Hell up through ducts to the hell above,

then using the handle of the shovel to slam
the cast-iron door in the face of circumstance. ~

Two new messes so far this week
and I think of the saddest life I've known

not the most tragic but the saddest
swept along in private humiliation

towards a death that still seems outsized.
I once believed he was brave or heroic;

now I see how circumstance numbed
him too much for self-pity or even self-regard.

At night I take pen and paper to bed
where I can find them without coming awake.

The flesh reposes but the spirit's taut
trying to exist a few moments in two dimensions at once

making notes in a round childish hand
that I hope will stay legible until morning.

Without the painful struggle, texts vanish
leaving moods to format the day,

not fragmentary records built up slowly,
old business carried forward from previous

meetings now rising to the head of the agenda.
The camera takes good care of

those it knows have the personality needed
for 1935, going to adventure

if adventure wouldn't come to him,
in the first car he ever owned

the heap the wreck the bus
at his best during the worst, at his zenith

during everyone else's nadir and out of step thereafter.
What about the early affair with that woman Lucille

who lived above a movie house?
She pitted him against a rival, a gladiatorial

contest to see whose foolhardiness would have her.
Drunk he crawled out to the point

of the triangular marquee, returning with
the distant-most bulb in his mouth like a clown's red nose:

the stuff of young guys who still had time to waste
rather than be wasted by.

Once much later, married to someone
whose parents and siblings all liked him but

shook their heads and maybe cried to see
her personality degrade so quickly

for one still so young herself.
Wartime prosperity and a first child come

perhaps a little scary for someone twenty-six
yet the spiral already past its apex.

Peace brings poverty. Friends lapse awkwardly

with the stories of her insults, feuds, apprehended

violence even when sober
which was less and less often and he withdrew to

escape? find peace? mourn much as I do now:
his auto-elegy for a life strangely disconnected

from the person living it,
yet running out all the same

like that of some artist kept in the dark
about his own intentions

forced never to forget a hundred and
twenty megabytes of amnesia? ~

The gauge maker was an artist
superior to the tool-and-die men

who lorded it over Singer, a simple
assembly line machinist

who had only the janitor to look down on
but didn't (the janitor

was a friend). Snobbery at the bottom
was different from that he went home to.

She never figured out anything, couldn't
be taught, despised people in

"new brick houses that cost twenty thousand"
hated everybody.

One of my earliest memories is of hearing
him discuss the war in Korea with a neighbour,

surprising because I was so small
extraordinary because he wasn't permitted

to talk to neighbours.
She fought with all those who'd made

better decisions in life, condescended
to the others like herself because

after all she'd married so well.
Korea looked bleak and so did the home front.

Singer, late thirties, jet black hair
combed straight back and parted in the middle,

two kids now but less of everything else
except what I imagine was the most quiet

kind of hope that ignored probabilities,
the logic of prospectors and gamblers,

but I don't truly know what he thought or dreamed
and that's my own little tragedy. ~

49

To the man running for president
outside the plant shaking hands

with everybody leaving the gate
Singer's felt no different than theirs,

no more lively, no less alive.
I knew him better by then,

forty-five, when the decay that inflated
also eroded,

slackening everywhere, thicker and thinner
at the same time, sagging chin,

eyes shutting down from the inside
from some wasting disease of a spirit that

nonetheless hadn't quite decided to concede:
in the several years remaining as

black-and-white wingtips grew antique in the closet
he took to sandals and a Basque beret

daydreaming with horrible urgency
of nostalgia never imagined or

needed until now.
Forty-five going on fifty-five but

at fifty-five, the age I am now, he'd been dead
quite long enough for this elegy to get underway.

Death was Singer's mid-life crisis.
He almost died that one time

like an elevator cage going into free fall
and the surprise of waking up

alive never left him.
Neither did the fear with which

he then suddenly had a relationship
but sometimes rebelled against in

unsure but unexpected ways.
Then the bell rang time's up.

Like most dying people he wanted to
be given an extension,

not a chance to rewrite everything back to the beginning.
When he admitted this couldn't be, he took

that answer with him as a last
minute addition to the small store of precious knowledge.

I don't believe he felt sorry for himself.
(Why start then? If storytelling actually tells

us anything, it's that death will confirm,
not contradict.) ~

Always more people to be mourned
always new people to grieve for them

but only so much feeling.
In charnel house days, the bones of

the freshly dead went in,
those of the others came out—

the ones of those no longer recalled even distantly.
In the end, it all has to do with memory

going forward not looking down
and then not glancing back.

But there's a great deal of this sorrow going round;
some of us catch it like the flu.

The elegy now like the eulogy then
does nothing for its subject

perhaps nothing for the listener either.
It once may have helped the devout

attenuate themselves to imagine they
saw the scene as the

dead themselves might do,
looking down knowingly, powerless, keeping

the link open. For a while it may help
blow air on recollection, making it lurch

in the fire it then becomes a part of,
warning of pain in some,

anaesthetising others: a matter of
temperament mostly

permitting us to evade
the memory but remember the elegist.

Tennyson tells us almost nothing about Hallam
whose existence we wouldn't know of otherwise

but something more of the writer himself
and so too here, I suppose:

a textbook example of
someone still alive with desire

starting to close
and no one to delegate the remembrance to

in an ever more accepting agony
for another born almost a century ago

and dead now nearly half as long:
the methodical pain of accident

extended mathematically forever
even after the last person who remembers

forgets and is himself or herself forgotten.
Elegies are funerals we conduct on paper to

make ourselves feel
better which, when temporary, survivors are welcome to

overhear, an ancient totally unsatisfying legacy
of the deaths that are suicides of a sort

and the others that are merely executions.
A prayer to the river gods might commence:

Please I can't die yet, there's
so much healing still to do.

That would be mine. Would it also
be his? I don't know how

we struggle on as we do when we can't
communicate more effectively than this. ~

The unembalmed body is that
of a fifty-one-year-old male caucasian

who checked out when the hotel needed the room.
Weight 165 pounds, length 68 inches.

The scalp once covered by thick black hair
betrays the scar inflicted by a beer stein

thrown across a nightclub in 1939 by
a stranger who later apologised.

The few remaining strands of hair fled to white
during the illness.

Lividity is everywhere. Eyes green
as always, lips light blue at present. A

slight ecchymotic patch is noted in the posterior aspect
of the body and throughout the entire narrative

of this life as blood collected in shallow pools
when times were tight or the pressure great

from unassumed ambition, duties that nagged,
responsibilities he refused to shake and messes

that couldn't be made to disappear.
There is a four-inch surgical scar in the lower right

quadrant of the abdomen arising from that time
he fell dead asleep at the Fairmont Hotel

after working thirty hours straight
and learned after waking with acute appendicitis

that the place had been evacuated an hour earlier.
Barely made it through on that occasion,

didn't survive the final emergency. No

one does. Petechiæ everywhere.

The lungs like the memory are clearly congested.
But there's no evidence of fluid in the mediastinum.

A lack of evidence characterises this case.
That and residual grief—to excess? who judges?

The heart weighs 10 ounces.
The oesophagus has a longitudinal fold,

the stomach contains the last breakfast,
the duodenum shows no ulcer

(miraculous when you think about it).
There is no gross abnormality

to speak of. There are no fracture lines
in clavicle, vertebrae, pelvic bones and so on.

The brain weighs 49 ounces.
Reflexion of the scalp reveals

no sign of haemorrhage or contusion.
Upon reflection I'm not sure

what to feel or
how to think about it. ~

59

Terra incognita was a disappointment
once discovered.

Let us search for some other dark place on the map.
If none is found then douse the lights

in some bright city and homestead there,
hole up as I believe he did

where everyone knew him but he wasn't found,
by which I mean engaged or distracted from the custom

of survival he followed until the end clamped
shut not suddenly but too soon.

Each day followed hard upon the last.
Disappointment always dwarfed success

for the ongoing failures were basic, the
triumphs small and quick, almost illusory

some of the time but kept alive in private thoughts
hidden where no one else would think to look.

His own Byzantium left no ruins,
not even faint outlines visible on the ground

for scholars to study and point out where living
people once walked where we walk now.

All of us inhabit these same odd spaces
where impressions outlive figures.

Snapshots we're holding turn archival in our hands
as the flesh of our fingers rots away.

Here we go back underground
actions rising from beneath the earth to greet

us midway.
Now we dismiss ourselves. Farewell

to valediction itself.
Life wasn't slick, it was dry.

He predeceased the city
though the monument was already tumbling.

People carried away bits as souvenirs,
thrilled by little larcenies as by almost nothing else.

I watched his eyes cross off each day
when he looked at the calendar in the kitchen.

At the start of every month he was brushed with hope,
odds and precedent notwithstanding.

At the end of every one he ripped down the page
and tore it into squares with a straightedge.

"I've gotta put this down on scratch paper."
But did he ever? I saw his mechanical pencil

write in lettering learned in drafting class years earlier,
before the Collapse of everything

but I never got to read the messages

He threw away the pages once he used them

to remind himself of secrets
until one day, one month, one year, fate far less subtle

than a meaty dream came due.
Events decayed and he ran out of life,

that's all. The only version was in the
imagination I seem to have inherited:

this was his bequest to me and
is now my surest reminiscence. ~

At the centre of the city is the cemetery where the dead
assemble to mock us with superior numbers and neatly

crosshatched streets and alleys, but there's no
direct route from the polished granite neighbourhood ("ritzy")

to the poor slate ones the wind plunders of statistics.
The graveyard city is a scandalous attack on what we know

passing itself off as satire.
My best excuse for why I didn't write this long ago

is that I've spent all these years in transit
to get past the shock I can't forget and

outstay this most superficial grief;
what I can't overcome is the loss I feel even more sharply

as he recedes and I follow, the way generations are intended to do
by the process that deposits us back at the basics

against our will. No wonder we're in turmoil all the time.
Hard as I tried to save it, I have forgotten the voice,

remembering merely its irony and gentleness,
but not the rest, for I seem to inhabit his appearance

like a suit of someone else's clothes
and this pleases me and terrifies in equal measure

often and especially right before sunrise.
The truth may be that the body is designed for fifty years'

hard use with no intermission. If so, he beat the odds
by a margin heartbreakingly spare to perform a death

that made so little difference to the map
that the characters still standing at the bar down the street

couldn't remember him or recognise the name
a short twenty years later when I sneaked in

for a fast bit of homage and a bitter glass of beer:
a life, that is, more interim than most or many or some,

hobbled by left-side vulnerability and conditions ambient
in the world, but not failed by any means, I've learned,

for he was wiser, kinder, still more tolerant, more
tranquil with the momentum that carries us along

more of everything at the close than at the start,
though events and sensations were rushed

towards the end, as the day reached the point it reaches
and he thanked those who protected him until he died

and life for me began in earnest;
he passed it to me like a baton in a relay race

and it cripples me to realise how little I've done.
I sweat tears to think about it and him; the two are no longer distinct.

I've read the literature of this wretched devastation
but feel nothing I haven't already said myself

expressed in my own arid idioticon
waiting for streetcars that don't exist. ~   65

Keats carried off
by tuberculosis, in Italy of course,

aet. twenty-eight it goes without saying:
Shelley remembered.

With Milton's Cambridge friend
too the lungs died first.

The Irish Sea displaced the air
inside them. You understand

I'm not comparing poets but subjects
who were topics of grief.

Who cares about the dead
white foreigners? Who leaves who behind?

Metaphor is my way of remaining in denial.
There was a history of death in the family.

He was let out early because of the holiday.
He never regained unconsciousness.

Death is the night clerk with the evil
grin who sneaks into your room and

slips beneath the covers beside you.
Prepare my bill, I've a train to catch;

it's chilly out and the long hall carpet
is worn down the centre

from feet all going in the same direction.
We anthropomorphise death while it

does the opposite to us. I've always
admitted the process. What I resisted was

that this death too soon was also
one so very long ago.

Then as now, people needed
all their luck simply to survive

and his leeched away.
The early Forties were his time but not

without trouble, like my Nineties;
in this and other ways we overlapped.

For all the unsaid conversations
and confidences never consummated,

this dead white foreigner and I were a team;
I succeeded in a series, neatly,

while the sequence of his own scenes failed him
like everything else.

The arc ended before it touched
the ground;

its errands done, the body moved
away and left me less as well.

If death doesn't kill you then something else will.
Forces are at work.

Some dyings are so gradual we think ourselves alone
but this was a sudden faltering, a quick deceleration

that speeded up things alarmingly.
No chance to shed confusions in old age.

He didn't seek the theory in things
but only in healing resignation.

He didn't cling to news to prove he was alive
and the death-worries helped to grind him

down to the finest ash.
His life, my times—I enjoy them.

Past and present are inseparable. Yes I know.
But with him gone I was really on my own

and now that I've lived far longer than he did
I find I've forgotten so much.

The words are not juried. I write
to verify how from the day it happened

I mourned but not always
in the same way or consistently, the grief

mutating as I wore on.
Splinters navigating through the loss

still move towards daylight and
poke through the skin unexpectedly.

I know I am selfish to mourn this way,
to trade on absence hoping for sympathy.

Such is the conceit of the survivor pro tempore
safe in his comfort and irritation

struggling to transcend.
He didn't go gentle into the good night exactly

but retained his subdued optimism
as the reasons for it failed him.

He didn't rail and didn't acquiesce
but let himself be overtaken

quickly but looking beyond the day
like someone who feels a cold coming on

and is resigned to rest and liquids,
relishing the time to think.

I write andante of one whose life
had little you could call allegro.

No one's been in to make the beds. ~

70

The Singer who is the subject of the poem is George Singer Fetherling, *obit* mcmlxvi. He was a part-involuntary exile from the polite and prosperous middle class, a charming and congenial man who for all that just wanted to be left alone. The Depression ended his education but in another sense began it. He worked as a kind of shop-floor samurai to a large industrial firm, then as a salesman, finally as a machinist of the lowest rank: the trend was always downward. He was a pleaser and a natural conciliator; he became the president of his union's local; everyone liked him except the person to whom he was tragically married. He was the father of two children, of whom the author is one.

The figure referred to as Herschel is Singer's father, Herschel Fetherling (1868-1938), an engineer, adventurous in his youth, who became an independent business person. He was separated from his son by the fact that he always remained a Victorian homme d'affaires, with codes and styles that seemed stiff and unforgiving in the twentieth century, while Singer was a modernist, thoroughly urban, bound to big machines, his internal life shaped by the Depression and his external one by the Second World War. Herschel too was an individual in possession of more than the usual numbers of secrets about himself.

As much as this is an elegy, "Singer" is also a requiem delivered at the long drawn-out funeral of the elegy as a literary form. Such poems of lament for the dead were once conspicuous in, for example, English literature. One alluded to in "Singer" is "Lycidas" by John Milton, written in memory of his friend Edward King who drowned in 1637. Another is "Adonais" by Percy Bysshe Shelley, composed on the death of another Romantic poet, John Keats, in 1821. Also mentioned in the preceding pages is "In Memoriam" by Lord Tennyson, which tries to plumb Tennyson's grief over the loss of his friend Arthur Henry Hallam, who at the time of his death in 1833 was engaged to marry the poet's sister. "Thyrsis" by Matthew Arnold, published in 1867 in memory of Arthur Henry Clough, another poet and fellow school administrator, is also classic of the once-famous sort, which might easily have been referred to in the text but isn't. "In Memoriam" is no doubt the example that still survives in curricula. Such poems have virtually nothing in common with Thomas Gray's "Elegy in a Country Churchyard" (1751), which probably began the debasing of *elegy* to cover verse that is merely excessive in its melancholy.

This poem had its origins in a dream I had in Chongqing in the Chinese province of Sichuan on the night of May 14/15, 1990. I began working on it in 2001 while writer-in-residence at the University of New Brunswick in Fredericton and completed it in 2003 while writer-in-residence at Berton House in Dawson, Yukon Territory. I am grateful to both these institutions.

George Fetherling is a poet, novelist, travel writer and
visual artist. He lives in Vancouver.